Ramayana Advayam

ISBN 979-8-88883-991-1

Ramayana Advayam

LATE BRAHMA-SRI R. VISVANATHA SASTRIGAL
(WITH ENGLISH TRANSLATION BY
PROF. V. KRISHNAMURTHY)
AUTHOR OF GITA-MRITA-MAHODADHI
(PUBD. BY SAMSKRITA ACADEMY MADRAS, 2018)

INDICACADEMY

CONTENTS

A BIOGRAPHICAL NOTE ABOUT THE AUTHOR (BY HIS SON)

Sri R. Visvanatha Sastrigal (1882-1956) worked in the judicial department of South Arcot district in the erstwhile Madras province of British India and retired as Subcourt Sheristadar, Cuddalore, in 1939. In his younger days, round about the 2nd decade of the 20th century, when he was working in Tirukkoilur and Cuddalore, every year (probably for four or five years) during the summer recess of two months, sending his wife and children to her father's place, he went over to Ganapathy Agraharam in Tanjore District to be for day and night at the lotus feet of Sri Sri Vasudeva Brahmendra Saraswati and stayed there like a gurukulavasi. He had all his Bhashya Pathas this way. This Acharya attained Samadhi on 4th March 1931.

My father left 27 original manuscripts expounding the advaita school and its symbiosis with Bhakti. Of these, Gitamritamahodadhi is the longest. This one, Ramayana advayam, is the shortest. Most of his manuscripts have now been deposited with Kuppuswamy Sastri Research Institue, Mylapore, Chennai.

During his lifetime my father gave numerous lectures, several saptAhas of Shrimad Bhagavatam and navAhas of

Valmiki Ramayana. One such event is recalled by him as a special note in his autobiographical writings. In the early thirties (in Octber 1934) he gave a fifteen day exposition of the Bhagavatam at the Manikarnika ghat in Varanasi in the beatific presence of His Holiness the Kamakoti Shankaracharya Sri Sri Chandrasekharendra Saraswati Swamigal (now known as the Kanchi Paramacharya) who was then on his first all-India tour.

RÂMÂYANA – ADVAYAM
BY SRI R. VISVANATHA SASTRI

(With Apologies to the author: The attempt at translation has been done by V. Krishnamurthy, the son of the author. At some places the translation does not seem to catch the insight of the original. It is hoped this will provide a challenge for researchers in the field)

PART – 1

Aum gam vânîm gurum natvâ vakshye râmâyanâdvayam |
šrî râmo hyayyate yatra svânanyah purushottamah ||1||

Om. Making obeisance to Ganesa, Sarasvati and the Guru, I narrate Ramayana-advayam (the non-duality enshrined in the Ramayana) wherein pervades Sri Rama the supreme personality, non-different from the Self.

Râma eva param brahma râma eva param tapah |
râma eva param satyam râmân nâsty anyad adbhutam ||2||

Rama is the transcendental Brahman; Rama is the supreme (goal of all) Penance; Rama is the Absolute Truth; other than Rama there is nothing significant.

Šricakre triputîrupe râjamânam ca yan mahah |
ayodhyâyâm devapuryâm râm jyotir nirgunam param ||3||

He shines as the effervescence in the three-fold form of the Sri Chakra (of the Goddess) and as the formless Supreme (single-syllable) RAM in the City Divine of Ayodhya (namely, the human body).

Svântasthanagarî daivî manah padme cidambare |
svîyajyotir veshtiteti šri râmah šaranam mama ||4||

My refuge is Sri Rama who dwells in his own divine city, (namely) my inner Mind, in the (lotus) space of Consciousness, radiating it by His own Light.

Šrimatpanchâksharajyoti<u>h</u> râmo jnânamaya<u>h</u> šiva<u>h</u> |
advaitânandamagnasya nânâtvam našyati dhruvam ||5||

Rama is the glory of the five-syllabled mantra (panchakshara) shining as Siva, the fullness of Knowledge. When one is immersed in this bliss of non-duality, the multiplicity of the world vanishes without fail.

Râmeti dvyaksharo mantra<u>h</u> panchâsh<u>t</u>âksharasârata<u>h</u> |
sarvâdhikârasiddhyartham vihita<u>h</u> kalitârakah ||6||

The two-syllabled mantra, namely, RA-MA, is the quintessance of both the five-lettered *(mantra of Siva)* and the eight-lettered (mantra of Narayana) ones. It has been prescribed (as the panacea) for crossing the darkness of the Kali and for the achievement of every purpose.

Râmânanyat prabhâ sîtâ labdhâ paulastyahânata<u>h</u> |
râva<u>n</u>oVhamk<u>r</u>ti<u>h</u> sâkshât tajjayo râmabâ<u>n</u>ata<u>h</u> ||7||

Rama, than whom His Power (=Ray of Light) Sita is not different. She was redeemed by vanquishing Ravana. Ravana is none else but Ego personified (in each one of us). Victory over that Ego is possible only by the use of the Rama arrow (that is, the name, Rama).

Mâyaiva d<u>r</u>šyate loke mâyi râmašca dehaga<u>h</u> |
g<u>r</u>hâyodhyânirgatašca svâsritadvaitašântida<u>h</u> ||8||

Mâyâ – is what we see (everywhere) in the Universe. The Magician (who owns the Maya) is Rama himself, who is the indweller of this body (of ours). Coming out of the City (=cave of the heart) of Ayodhya He bestows peace from duality to those who seek refuge.

*Yat*pâduke samâšritya bharato râshtrapâlakah |
Mâyâtyâgî mohahantâ vivekašaranam gatah ||9||

Yat, – meaning, He, whose sandals were obtained by Bharata, makes a King of the latter. He renounces Mâyâ (i.e., Sita), kills Delusion (=Moha, that is, Maricha) and takes refuge in Discretion (that is, Sugriva)

*Na*syâvatârâh kapayah sîtânveshana udyatâh |
setau lingam ca sampûjya svasmin rakshâmsi hanti ca ||10||

Na – meaning, Siva and His ganas, have reincarnated as the host of monkeys. They spread out everywhere looking for Sita (and succeeded). (Rama) worships the Siva Lingam at the seashore and kills the Rakshasas (Evil) in Oneself.

*Ma*kâro mangalam vakti svârâjyašrîpradas-tathâ |
Mânishâdeti[1] mantrena manasi sthâpyate harih ||11||

Ma – the syllable that speaks of a prosperous ending and bestows the Wealth of Self-hood. And one establishes this in the Mind by the mantra beginning with Mâ-nishâda (the initial shloka which was the harbinger of Valmiki's Ramayana).

Etam râmâyanam mantram vedasâram ca muktidam |
guror labdhvâ ca vâlmîkih gâyethâm iti šishyakau ||12||

This Ramayana Mantra, which is the essence of the Vedas, which bestows Release (from Samsara) was got from the Preceptor (Narada) by Valmiki and was transmitted to his two disciples for being sung (aloud in the world).

**Abravîn madhuram geyam iti coditavân r̲shih̲ |
ramâyanârnave magnau vâlmîkir nârado'pi ca ||13||**

Sing it sweet, preached the Sage. Valmiki as well as Narada were immersed to the brim in the ocean(-like bliss) of Ramayana.

**Sthitaprajnasusamvâde tasyaiva caritam madhu |
vân̲îkat̲âkshâd udbhutâm *vâcam artho'nudhâvati*[2] ||14||**

Out of this blessed conversation about the Man of confirmed wisdom (Sthita-prajna) arose the honey-like history of Him (Rama) by the divine grace of Goddess Saraswati. The words flowed first. Meaning followed suit.

**Tapasvinošca samvâdât tapasvî câdhikâry api |
vijijnâsasva tapasâ ceti šruty anušâsanam ||15||**

From the words of the Tapasvi – ascetic who had the power and strength of Askesis (=tapas) – the listener who was equally a tapasvi received the message. 'Realise (Brahman, for yourself, by yourself) by tapas', says the Vedic Commandment.

**Karmabhaktim ca vâlmikih vašisht̲o jnânam ûcivân |
prâcetasau munî chettham *vedam râmâyanâtmanâ*[3] ||16||**

Creator Brahma's progenies Valmiki and Vasishta – one wrote about Karma and Bhakti and the other spoke about Jnana. Thus were the Vedas (rejuvenated) through the form of Ramayana.

**Âkhyâtavantau lokârtham šreyase svahitâya ca |
advaitam paramam tattvam parokshârthatayâ svatah̲ ||17||**

Both for the benefit of mankind and for their own good, they have narrated the Absolute Truth of non-duality, (sometimes) subtly and (sometimes) directly.

Ahamkâravadhâyaiva tapasotpâditam maha_h_ |
šrirâmajyotir advaitam grastam râva_n_arâhu_n_â ||18||

For the fall of Ego did the Supreme Light of Rama emanate from the tapas (of men and divines alike). The non-dual Sun of Rama was (for a while) eclipsed by serpent Rahu in the form of Ravana.

Ahamkâramanorajye sareshâm kun_thi_tho gati_h_ |
dehâtmadhîr ahamkâra_h_ sarvadukhasya kâra_n_am ||19||

While Ego has its sway, man's mind seeks crooked paths. Ego is nothing but the notion: 'I am the body' and this is the cause of all misery.

Jahi šatrum mahâbâho[4] **yo râtîyati tam jahi |**
daharastham harim jnâtvâ buddhau šara_n_am ishyate ||20||

Vanquish this enemy of yours. That which creates obstacles must be conquered by you. Realise the Lord who lives in the confines of the heart and surrender to the (Cosmic) intellect. This is the prescription.

Guhâyodhyâ durlabheti tad daršanam abhîpsitam |
kešavas tatparo râma_h_ ardhanârîš vara_h_ prabhu_h_ ||21||

The City of Ayodhya in the cave (of the heart) is difficult to be accessed. To view it is the ambition. The in-dweller is the Lord Rama (none other than), Kesava, (and) the half-feminine Iswara.

Kalâtîtâ bhagavatî râme_n_a ca saha svasâ |
lakshmanašca kalârûpah akâro višvabhâvana_h_ ||22||

The Goddess Sita along with her (shadow) sister (Godess Ambika)[5], transcends all kalâs. Lakshmana is the form of kalâ, the form of the syllable A (the first syllable of Aum), the form of Višva (in the three-fold višva-taijasa-prâjna Cosmic manifestation).

Nâdasvarupo bharata̱h makâra̱h prâjnarûpaka̱h |
bindusvarûpa̱h šatrugna̱h ukâras taijasâtmakah ||23||

Bharata is nâda, the syllable ma and prâjna. Satrugna is bindu, the syllable u and taijasa.

Šivo makâro hanumân ukâro harinâyaka̱h |
akâro jâmbavân âtmâ brahmâmša iti cerita̱h ||24||

Hanuman is Siva and the syllable ma (of Aum). Sugriva is the syllable U. Jambavan, the physical spark from Creator Brahma is the syllable A.

AumkâroSsht̲âksharah sûkshma̱h râmo nârâyano nara̱h
bhuvo vi̱t sûkshmadarši ya̱h svatattvam vettum arhati ||25||

The mantra Aum is the subtle essence of the eight-syllabled mantra. It is Rama, it is Narayana. He who gets to the residual substratum of the Universe deserves to know the Self-Principle.

Janmântare kašyapo yo devapû rakshitâ hi sah |
tasyâšvamedhe šrivish̲nu̱h upayâto'bhayaprada̱h ||26||

He who was Kasyapa in a previous birth – Kasyapa who protected the divine kingdom – in his Aswamedha sacrifice the Lord Vishnu, decided to bestow Abhaya (Fearlessness).

Devâstam šara̱nam prâpya dvaitâd vîtabhayâ̱h kshanât |
yo'sau sarvagato vish̲nu̱h mahâsattâ svarûpatah ||27||

The divines gave themselves up to Him as the only refuge – Him who is the ultimate Grand Reality and who permeates and pervades everything and everywhere. In a moment they were rid of the Fear of Duality (i.e. Fear of the world outside).

Advaitâ brahma<u>n</u>a<u>h</u> šakti<u>h</u> mâyâ pâtrîm samâšritâ |
pâyasâtmâ dravîbhûtâ *etâš chatašraschaturdhâ*[6] **||28||**

The Power of Brahman is unique. It was materialised as a magic vessel containing the spiritual essence in liquid form. This became divided into four parts.

Brahmopanayanât pašcât vâšish<u>th</u>ašrava<u>n</u>e ratâ<u>h</u> |
kartâ bahir akartânta<u>h</u> loke vicara râghava[7] **||29||**

After the ritual of Upanayana which leads (the way) to Brahman they were all engaged in listening to the teaching of Vasishta. Action outside, but untouched inside by action, thus move in the world, Rama, – (was the teaching of Vasishta).

Ityevamupadish<u>t</u>oVpi svanish<u>th</u>âyâšca notthithah |
svapûrnâtmâtireke<u>n</u>a jagajjîvešvarâdaya<u>h</u> ||30||
Na santy ajnânakâryâ<u>n</u>i râm jyotishi katham tama<u>h</u> |
iti vijnânasampanna<u>h</u> pašyannapi na pašyati ||31||

Even though they were taught thus, (Rama) did not wake up from his Samadhi in the Self. Outside of the Atman within Oneself, there is neither the universe nor the jiva because they are the effects of Ignorance. In the effervescence of Rama, how can darkness (arise)? Endowed with this practical wisdom he does not see, even though seeing!

Evam râma<u>h</u> sthithaprajna<u>h</u> tam câlayitum âgata<u>h</u> |
višvâmitro mahâtejâh devai<u>h</u> protsâhito muni<u>h</u> ||32||

It was such a Rama – the man of confirmed wisdom – who was iintended to be disturbed by the coming of Visvamitra the great sage, who was (himself) prodded by the divines.

Višvam mithyeti vijnâya vijno drashtâ svavistrtim |
svamâtradarší samyagjnah rshir yogešvaro munih ||33||

The Sage (Visvamitra) was an adept in Yoga; knows well; sees the Self and Self only; realising that the visible universe is only an appearance, sees His own Self in all its fullest expansion (as the Universe itself).

Aham brahmaiva râmo'smi iti svam paripašyati |
mahâvâkyair vedagîrbhih vyashtyahamkâravân na hi ||34||

I am Brahman. I am Rama – thus does one see oneself rightly, (as taught) by the Grand Pronouncements (of the Upanishads) and the music of the Vedas. The Individual is not the Ego or the egoist.

Avyayam bhâvam evaikam[8] **pašya sarvatra sarvadâ |**
matputro râma ity eva mamatâm hi parityaja ||35||

See the One Imperishable every time and everywhere. This is my son Rama - is an attitude of possession. This should be discarded.

Mahatmâyam sarvalokašaranya iti câbravît |
munivâkyam satyam iti vašishtho'numumoda ca ||36||

The words of the sage, namely, this (Rama) is a Mahatma; he is the refuge of the entire universe, – were confirmed as true by Vasishta.

Râjadattakumârâbhyâm devapûh prasthito munih |
balâm atibalâm câpi grâhayâmâsa šâstratah ||37||

The Sage left for the divine city along with the two princes handed over by the King. They assimilated from him in the due manner (the two Mantras): balâ and atibalâ.

Kâmâśrame japan sandhyâm śaktim gu_namayîm iti |
puna_h punaš ca sandhyoktih_ dvaitavismarana_âya hi ||38||

They did the *sandhyopasana* in the hermitage known as Kamasrama. *Sandhya* is the manifest Power (of the Unmanifest). (In the Ramayana) there is mention of *sandhya* again and again. Indeed this is for the eradication of duality (in the mind).

Šâpât prâptâh pâpayonim bodhayanty eva câdvayam |
šâpân muktâ api svam svam divyarûpam prapedire ||39||

The evil births were obtained (by the Rakshasas) because of a spell. This only confirms (the principle of) non-duality. Once released from the spell (by the arrows of Rama) they got back their own divine forms.

Iti dr_šyasya mithyâtvam tejorûpasya satyatâ |
upatasthur mantradevâh_ mahâtmânam ca râghavam ||40||
Mânasâ me bhavishyadhvam ity advaitam parâmr_tam |
siddhâśramasthaviprâ hi snânasandhyâjapâdibhih_ ||41||

Thus was confirmed the illusoriness of the visible universe and the reality of the Glorious Effervescence. The gods of the mantras worshipped Rama, the Mahatma. The sages of the Siddhasrama by their rituals of bath, sandhyopasana and japa, prayed to reach this non-dual supreme nectar.

Gangâvatarana_âkhyânaśravana_ât padyate ca yat |
purastât triputtî jyotih_ sarvatrânubhavanti te ||42||

They experienced the three-fold Glory, that which is reached by listening to anecdotes like the Descent of Ganga, right in front of them.

Âdhâracitsamudrâcca rašmimân udayaty aho |
jâhnavî saritâ šres<u>th</u>â hy uttamâ vrittir ucyate ||43||

From the Ocean of Consciousness at the base does the One with the (glorious) rays rise. Indeed the great river Ganges stands for the noblest attitude (of mind).

Satyâdi sarva lokeshu nistraigu<u>n</u>yam param padam |
gu<u>n</u>atîtam gamayati tejomayašarîrakam ||44||

Among the various worlds starting from Satyaloka, it takes one to the Absolute State, a state of effervescence, devoid of the three gunas, beyond the gunas.

Šivašaktyâtmakam teja<u>h</u> skândam advaitam îritam |
sha<u>d</u>ânana<u>h</u> kârtikeya<u>h</u> sha<u>t</u>cakreshu ca gîyate ||45||

The Light of Skanda, the soul of Siva-sakti, brings out the concept of non-duality. (That is why) the six-faced Kartikeya is praised in the six cakras (of the yogic body)

Sadâbrahmamayî vritti<u>h</u> yatprasâdâcca labhyate |
manasturagam âlabhya câšvamedha<u>h</u> pade pade ||46||

By His Grace does one get the attitude of mind which is always fixed in Brahman. (From that stage) every step is an asvamedha yajna, the mind being the sacrificial horse.

Manonmanî manonâšât jnânânandam<u>r</u>todadhi<u>h</u> |
šrirâmâr<u>n</u>avam advaitam sarvam râmamayam jagat ||47||

Once the mind is vanquished and extinguished the nectar-like ocean of bliss arising from Enlightenment (shows only) the non-dual wave of Sri Rama flooding the entire universe.

Yajnîyam pašum âlabhya manonigraha ishyate |
manasturagamedhena pûrsho yajnamayo bhavet ||48||

The sacrificial cow is the mind. It is the removal of the mind that is desired. In this grand horse-sacrifice (Aswa-medha) the Purusha becomes himself the yajna.

Yajnaghnavrittihananam višvâmitrasahâyata<u>h</u> |
mitro hi yajnapurusha<u>h</u> cidraviŝcaikavimšaka<u>h</u> ||49||

The attitudes of mind which obstruct the path of Yajna have to be destroyed with the help of Visvâmitra. Mitra the Sun is the Yajna-Purusha. The Sun of Consciousness is 21-fold.

Tadupâstyâca tatteja<u>h</u> anusandhîyate'nišam |
Tejovriddhi<u>h</u> sadâbhyâsât viraso bâhyavastushu ||50||

By worshipping the Sun that Infinite Light is meditated upon daily. All interest is gone in external things. Constant practice (this way) multiplies one's (spiritual) Power.

Sandhyâvidyâsamudita<u>h</u> šrirâma<u>h</u> paramam maha<u>h</u> |
kalyâ<u>n</u>arâmarûpe<u>n</u>a drash<u>t</u>um aiccan mahâmuni<u>h</u> ||51||

Sri Rama, the Absolute, coupled with the Light of Sandhya, was now desired to be seen in His (delightful) marital form by the great sage.

Kausalyâ suprajâ[9] **iti jagatpitrošca vaibhavam |**
pratyaksham anubhûyeha mithilâm prasthito muni<u>h</u> ||52||

The muni (Visvamitra) had a direct experience of the glory of the Father of the Universe, through (the episode of waking up Rama by) the sloka 'Kausalya supraja (rama)'. Then he set off for Mithila.

Yatraisha jagadâbhâsa<u>h</u> drash<u>t</u>avyas tatra râghava<u>h</u> |
ato jyâyân hi purusha<u>h</u> itîre naravigrahâ<u>h</u> ||53||
Striya eveti niścitya rajodoshayutâ iti |
nistraigu<u>n</u>yam yadadvaitam vedyam divyam amûrtakam ||54||

Wherever there is appearance of universe, Rama has to be seen there. The Purusha is therefore supreme. Men are only men in form; they are women because they are defaulted by rajo-guna. What is non-dual and devoid of the three gunas is the Divine that is formless.

Yajnakun<u>d</u>âd udgatam ca râmatejomayam b<u>r</u>hat |
Yajnabhûmer utthitâ ca sîtâ śaktitrayâtmikâ ||55||

The great fullness of splendour that is Rama arose from the sacrificial pot (of Pâyasa). The personality of Šakti, that is a three-in-one form as Sita, also rose from the sacrificial land, (the land that was being tilled for Yajna).

Sîteti vângmayî kanyâ sambhûtâ vedadhârane |
sâkshâd vedavatî nâmnâ brahmajnânaprabheti sâ ||56||

The Damsel of Speech manifested as Sita for the purpose of rejuvenating the Vedas. She was in fact known as Vedavati. She is nothing but the Splendour of Brahman-Enlightennment.

Yanmaya<u>h</u> purusha<u>h</u> sâkshât sarvabhûtah<u>r</u>di sthitah |
svânubhuty ekamânena pra<u>n</u>avas tasya vâcaka<u>h</u> ||57||

That Absolute Fullness has expressed itself in the hearts of everything living. To experience it directly one resorts to the Pranava (the syllable Aum) as Its vocal expression.

Šrîrâmatâpanîyârthajyotîrâma iti šruta_h_ |
smr̥te sakalakalyân̠abhâjanam yatra jâyate ||58||

The splendour of Rama (both the word and the personality indicated by the name) is talked about in Sri-Rama-tapani (Upanishad). By the mere memory (of that name) one partakes of everything that is good.

Videho hi mahâjnânî tâvevam ghaṭayaty athom |
ayonijâyâ vishn̠ošca vivâhe kr̥tavân pan̠am ||59||

The great seer, King Janaka, brought the two together and in the marriage of Sita and Rama really created a turning point (in the history of the universe).

Sîtâbhimânaputrîti šrirâmâya tad arpan̠ât |
sarvatrâbhimatîm tyaktvâ svamâtram avašishyate ||60||

(The act of Janaka in) giving away his favourite daughter to Sri Rama (indicates) the renunciation of the Ego or Possessiveness in everything and resting in One's Self alone.

Advaitaparamâm šântim labdhvâ cânyan na pašyati |
gûḍham ca vângmayam jyotih nâdabrahman̠i lîyate ||61||

Having obtained the Absolute Peaceful State, one does not perceive anything else. The subtle splendour of the Fullness of Speech merges in Nâda-Brahman.

Saha svasâmbikâ sîtâ châyevânugatâ sadâ |
šaktišaktimatoraikyam yathâ candrasya candrikâ ||62||

Sita was always (subtly) accompanied by the sister-Goddess Ambika, like a shadow. The Sita-Rama marriage was the (inseparable) union of Energy and the Energiser, like the moonlight with the moon.

Šrîrâmasannidhâne ca jâmadagnyo ja<u>d</u>ikr̥ta<u>h</u> |
eko deva<u>h</u> satyasatyam ity advaitam parâmr̥tam ||63||

In the presence of Sri Rama the son of Jamadagni (i.e., Parasurama) was immobilised. The truth of truths is that there is only One Divinity. This supreme blissful fact of Non-duality (is vindicated).

Akshayo madhuhanteti râma evânumodita<u>h</u> |
***râma<u>h</u> satpurusho loke*[10] anye kâpurushâ matâ<u>h</u> ||64||**

Rama alone has been applauded as the Imperishable and Madhu-hanta (the destroyer of Madhu). In the whole world Rama is the Sat-purusha (the ideal human being for emulation). All others are only miserable creatures.

Sahasrâdityasamkâšam sarvašatrunibarha<u>n</u>am |
râmašaktimayam bâ<u>n</u>am dhyâyed[11] vâ sarvatomukham ||65||

The One who looks like a thousand Suns, the one who devastates every one of the enemies, the one who has faces in all directions, such a powerful one is the arrow (of Rama)– that has to be meditated on.

Svajjyoti<u>h</u> sarvagam iti tatra šakti<u>h</u> pracodanam |
anyavrittîr nirasyaiva tanmayatvam iheshyate ||66||

One's inner lustre is the One that is pervading everywhere. This is what monitors the Power of the individual. All other tendencies are discarded. This attitude of one-ness (with the Absolute) is what is prescribed.

Svetarânâm vâsanânâm tiraskârena dhîradhîh |
pratyagjyotir vâsanayâ sadâ tishthati kevalah ||67||

The man of brave intellect discards all tendencies of the mind which take him away from the Self. He always stands rooted in the Self, the Self alone, through his conviction.

Satyam ekapadam brahma[12] **tatrâham api codaye |**
iti vânî ca kaikeyyâh advaite paryavasyati ||68||

I am prodding you on towards Satya, Truth, which is the single base of Brahman the absolute – says Kaikeyi (See V.R. 2-14-7) Even these words of Kaikeyi end up in Non-duality.

Devadevyor mantrasâram vijnâya narakesarî |
parvatâdiva nishkramya guhâyâm nihitah prabhuh ||69||

The Lion of Men understood the essentials of the discussion betrween the King and the Queen. The Lion (in Him) now came out (of its solitude of the Palace into the Open World) (as a lion comes out) of its hiding in the cave of the mountain.

Varâharudhirâbhena candanena sugandhinâ |
tam vaiśravanasamkâśam upapannam svatejasâ ||70||
Vajrâjinâdidhâri ca simho giriguhâśayah |
parjanyasûryacandrâdi tulyo'yam sarvatomukhah ||71||
Ityâdi rshivâkyâni avatâreshvamûrtakam |
ekam hi nirgunâdvaitam avâcyam ca vadanty aho ||72||

Lo and behold! how the Rishi Valmiki speaks of the formless form, of that which cannot be spoken by words, of the attributeless non-dual singleton! Wearing the red rudraksha stones and sweet smelling sandal-paste, by his own lustre he reached the status of Kubera. Though wearing the tiger-skin and the like, the lion of the mountain-cave, looked as if he, the one who faced everything, were Indra, the Sun and the Moon, etc.

Sarvalokâtigo'dvaitah lokaikašarano'vyayah |
yogišvaro râjarâjah sarvabhûtahrdi sthitah ||73||

He transcends all the worlds. He is non-dual. He is the only Refuge for all the worlds. He is imperishable. He is the Lord of Yoga. He is the King of Kings. He dwells in the hearts of everything that is living.

Dharmapâlo dharmamûrtih yenedam dhâryate jagat |
sarvân paurâns tiraskrtya turagâš coditâ yathâ |
tathâ dhîvrittayah sarvâh netavyâs svasukhe dhiyâ ||74||

Protector of Dharma, Personification of Dharma – by Him is the entire universe sustained. Such a One discarded the entire population of citizens (of Ayodhya) and prodded his horses away from them. So also do we have to lead our tendencies of the mind, by our intelligence, – all for the Self.

Vâgyatâste trayah sandhyâm ity advaitavibhâvanam |
vyavahârasya madhyepi ekabhâvâvagâhanam ||75||

Silent meditation of the Sandhya (devata or mantra) three times is a way of developing (the conviction of) non-duality. Even amidst all activities one should be (internally) immersed in the attitude of oneness.

Smâryate vaidikair dharmaih *nânyah panthâ*[13] iti šrutih |
jalâdimocanântepi bhojane šuchibhâshane ||76||
Advaitasmârakâ mantrâh âvartyante punah punah |
rshitulyaš citrakûte svâtmârâmo hy avasthitah ||77||

The Vedic religion keeps reminding you that there is no other way (for Release). During the process of eating or of social conversation or even at the end of (the daily duties of) excretion, etc., there are mantras, reminding one of Non-duality, which are repeated again and again. Thus like a sage, (Rama) lived in Chitrakuta, resplendent in His own Self.

Nirîkshya[14] **bharatah śrîmân prapadya** *gurum*[15] **advayam |**
tatpûjârtham svîkrtavân gurucoditapâduke ||78||

(This is the state in which) Bharata saw the Lord; (it was a divine sight!) He surrendered to the Lord-Guru to whom there was no equal. For His worship did he accept the sandals of the Lord, blessed unto him.

Caranau tau tu râmasya drakshyâmi saha pâdukau |
cidrašmir eva caranam tadyogam ca cidârnave ||79||
Prârthayan neva bharatah nandigrâme'vasat sudhîh |
nivedya pâdukâbhyâm ca râmâdvaitârnavam mahat ||80||

Those two lotus feet of Rama, I shall be seeing along with the sandals, so thought Bharata. The feet of the Lord are just the rays of Consciousness. Holding on to them is the union with the Ocean of Consciousness. Thus did the wise Bharata live in Nandigrama. Dedicating himself to the divine sandal-pair he was immersed in the great ocean of non-duality of Rama.

ENDNOTES FOR PART 1

[1] This expression *'Mânishâda'* is from the original Vâlmîki Râmâyana (V.R.). Here the sloka itself refers to the original. Here and elsewhere in this article, in the sloka portion, wherever there is a word or expression lifted straight from the scriptures – Râmâyana, the Gîta, the Bhâgavatam, the Upanishads, Yoga Vâsishtam, etc. –this fact will be indicated by giving the word or expression in italics, along with a footnote which gives the source of the word. Very often the use of such original expressions will be very significant for the understanding of this work. In fact most of the times a word or phrase is lifted from the original V.R., that word or phrase is pregnant with meaning, according to the commentators of the V.R. and the author of Râmâyana-Advayam does not obviously want to miss the pregnant words of the Âdi-kavi.

[2] Uttara-râma-caritam of Bhavabhuti

[3] Invocatory verses for the V.R.

[4] The Gita, III – 43.

[5] See also Sloka No.62.

[6] Yajur Veda

[7] Yoga Vâsishtam

[8] The Gita XVIII – 20

[9] V.R.1 -23 – 2 (Here and elsewhere in this article, all references to V.R. are to the *Valmiki Ramayana* ed. By T.R. Krishnamacharya, Nirnayasagara Press, Bombay, 1913)

[10] V.R.2 -2 29

[11] Compare with the following Dhyana-mantra for the ritual recitation of V.R.:

Sahasrâdityasamkašam sarvašatrunibarhanam

râmašaktimayam dhyâyed-yamogham Râmasâyakam.

[12] V.R. 2 – 14 – 7

[13] Purusha Sukta

[14] V.R. 2 – 99 – 25.See Footnote 15 below.

[15] V.R. 2-99-25. By using the two words 'nirikshya' and 'gurum' from this famous verse, the author subtly recalls all the pregnant meanings that commentators have built into this verse of V.R.

PART – 2

Yatra sarvâtmanâ majjan nânyam pašyati nânyathâ |
vaidehîm lakshmanam râmam adbhutam jnânavigraham ||81||
nistraigu_nyam tridhâ bhinnam d_rshtvâ ca paramarshay_ah |
d_ršyasya mâyikatvâcca mâyâtîtam param vidu_h ||82||

Where one is immersed in the fullness of the Absolute, one does not see anything else. Sita, Lakshmana and Rama together constituted a wonderful (integrated) form of Absolute Knowledge. The sages recognised this phenomenon as the formless one splitting itself into three forms. They realised the illusoriness of the visible and thereby the Reality of Transcendental One beyond the visible.

Antašca m_rgyam yat teja_h sarvato'pi prakâšate |
tatraiva d_rshticittâni ramante'nyânapekshayâ ||83||

That lustre which one seeks within oneself now shines everywhere. Their minds fixed therein they revel in that feast unmindful of anything else.

Advaitânandaparama_h iti tvam vidito mayâ |
Evam virâdhena coktam šarabhango mahân iti ||84||

You are the Absolute Bliss without equal, I have understood you, so said Viradha as also the great sage Sarabhanga.

Vaikhânasâ vâlakhilyâ_h samprakshâ_lâ marîchipâ_h[1] |
ašayyâ_h salilâhârâ_h ityâdi niyamânvitâ_h ||85||

**Advaitarâmasamprâptâ dan<u>d</u>akâranyavâsina<u>h</u> |
pûrnânande nimagnâśca bahir antastvarûpakâ<u>h</u> ||86||**

There were several types of Rshis living in the Dandaka forest; Those who were in their Vanaprastha-asrama; those who were created by Brahma in a dwarf form; those who were known for their ablution of all sins by water alone; Rshis who could absorb rays of light; those who needed no sleep; those who lived only on water; these and many more of different disciplines. But all of them had illumined themselves by the Rama-mantra which is the only non-dual Reality. They were totally immersed in the Absolute (themselves becoming) formless within and without.

Sukham nityam svaprakâśam *tejo dharme<u>n</u>a labhyate* |
dharmasâram jagaditi[2] *sîtâyodâh<u>r</u>tam*[3] **hitam ||87||**

The essence of Dharma is what sustains the Universe. Sita quoted this maxim in Her advice: Happiness, Eternity, Self-Enlightenment, and Glory all come only from Dharma.

Avyatha<u>h</u> kharahanteti *nâyam hanti na hanyate*[4] |
ity acchedyam param tattvam advaitam ca samîkshate ||88||

He was not hurt; he was the one who destroyed Khara. In reality (however), he neither kills nor is killed. This ultimate principle of being unaffected is what is indicated by non-duality.

Vaidehî lokamâteti rakshitâ svîya tejasâ |
râmo vigrahavân dharma<u>h</u>[5] **sandhyâ sîtâ ca tatprabhâ ||89||**

Sita being the Mother-Goddess of the entire universe, is protected by Her own Power. Rama is Dharma personified and Sita is the Light of that (Glory).

Advaitašrîrâmašakti<u>h</u> šakyâ dharshayitum na ca |
râmašakty âkrântam idam na tad asti na yatra sâ ||90||

The Rama-Power is unparalleled. It cannot be overpowered. This Universe is fully possessed by It. Nothing is there where that Power is absent.

Aprameyam hi tat teja<u>h</u> râmabhûtam idam vanam |
vrkshe vrkshe ca pašyâmi[6] **ity advaitânubhûr aham ||91||**
Mârîcenopadish<u>t</u>am yat tan na d<u>r</u>sh<u>t</u>am hi rakshasâ |
arâmadešam yah pašyet tasya mrtyu<u>h</u> kare sthita<u>h</u> ||92||

His lustre is unlimited. This entire forest is totally pervaded by Rama. I see Him in every tree, tree after tree, says Maricha. This is Advaita. But this advice given by Maricha was not taken by Ravana. He who sees without seeing Rama – such a one has his death imminent.

Râmavyâptajagaty eva caran šuddhim avâpsyati |
raghuvîra padadhyânam sarvatreha ca manga<u>l</u>am ||93||

Only by moving in the world of Rama's pervasion one obtains Purity. Meditation on the lotus feet of the King of Raghus augurs prosperity everywhere.

Sagu<u>n</u>e nirgu<u>n</u>am jyoti<u>h</u> sarvatrâpi prakâšate |
pašyan râmâya<u>n</u>am jyoti<u>h</u> ekam âlambanam param ||94||

The attributeless Light shines everywhere in that which has attributes. Seeing the Light of the Ramayana is the one ultimate prop.

Śrîrâmavancanodyuktau ubhau mâricarâkshasau |
kaivâsyeyam kart_rteti kâlapâsavašam gatau ||95||

The two, Marica and Ravana, were intent on fooling Sri Rama. Who is the architect of this Fate? They were both in the grip of (the God of) Death – Time.

Śrîsîtârâmacetâmsi âk_rshya balavân vidhi_h |
navagrahâ_nâm dâr_dhyâcca krîdatîty adbhutam mahat ||96||

Mighty Fate enveloped the minds of both Sri Sita and Sri Rama. This is a most wonderful feat of the might of the nine grahas.

Arûpam bhagavadrûpam rûpamity aupacârikam |
cidânandaghanam satyam tadvyâpyam nahi kutra cit ||97||
Vyâpyavyâpakatâ mithyâ svayam pûr_nasvarûpata_h |
pûr_navašeshašrutyâ ay a gaccati na tish_thati ||98||

God's Form is the formless form. The word 'form' itself is a conventional weakness of language. Truth is the fullness of Knowledge and Bliss. That cannot pervade anywhere, because, by its own fullness the talk of 'pervasion' and 'the pervaded one' is all false. Scripture talks of its Fullness, its Pervasion and also its Residual Fullness. This only indicates that Rama neither 'goes' nor 'stands' (in other words, Rama is untouched by his bodily actions).

Sa na kimcit karotîti mâyâmâtram hi d_ršyate |
mâyâ sarvatra hantavyâ tadasamsp_rsh_tacetasâ ||99||.

He does not do anything. What we see is only an illusory appearance. This illusion is to be destroyed – by a mind which is untouched by it.

**Adhish_thanâvašesho hi nâša_h kalpitavastuna_h |
iti nyâyas ca drash_tavya_h mârîcâdivadhâdapi ||100||**

Only the substratum survives. The imagined appearance is what dies. It is this logic that should be inferred from the killing of Marica.

**G_rhîtvâ pâyasam sîtâ indradattam ca mâyayâ |
kshuttr_dbâdhâ na lankâyâm maithilyâš ca kadâcana ||101||**

(In Lanka) Sita received from Indra, by a mâyâ as it were, a kind of drink by which she did not suffer from hunger or thirst (during her stay) in Lanka.

**Idam šarîram nissamjnam bandha vâ khâdayasva vâ |
tvayâ sprash_tum na šakyâ'smi iti sîtâ ca nirbhayâ ||102||
Pratyabhâshata lankešam *lokân nodvijate*[7] ca yâ |
svašakti j_rmbhitam lokam pašyantî râmapûritam ||103||**

Sita had no fear from anything in the world. Fearless as she was, She replied to the Lord of Lanka: You cannot touch me; you may imprison this inert body or even eat it. Her own spiritual power extends everywhere in the world which She saw as pervaded by Sri Rama.

***Naishâ pašyati râkshasya_h nemân pushpaphaladrumân |
ekasthah_rdayâ nûnam râmam evânupašyati*[8] ||104||**
**Ity ânjaneyavâkyam ca šuddhâdvaitasya bodhakam |
âsînah samvišans tish_than[9] kamso'dvaitam ca d_rsh_tavân ||105||**

Neither she sees the Rakshasis surrounding her, nor does she see the trees, fruits and flowers; keeping the One Thing in her heart, certainly she sees Rama alone everywhere.

This was the remark of Hanuman on sighting her for the first time. This teaches nothing but pure Advaita. (In the Bhagavatam, Kamsa) whether he was sitting, relaxing or standing also felt this non-duality by seeing Krishna everywhere.

LakshyavedheVpy arjuno hi ekabhâvasamâsthita<u>h</u> |
dehâdînâm vism<u>r</u>tiš ca bhaktai rapy anubhûyate ||106||

In hitting his mark, Arjuna exhibited this concentration on one and only one object. Forgetting one's own body is also experienced by intense devotees.

Âtmaikyajnânabhâvena kapaya<u>h</u> šivarûpi<u>n</u>a<u>h</u> |
gopâlâ gopikâš câpi yathâ dan<u>d</u>akavâsina<u>h</u> ||107||

The monkeys, by their attitude of the one-ness of the selves, were only Siva in different forms. So were the cowherds and cowherdesses of Gokulam, as also the sages of the Dandaka forest.

Šrîrâmadaršanam prâpya hy ara<u>n</u>ye pûtatâm gatâ<u>h</u> |
bahavo *bhâvitâtmâna<u>h</u>*[10] advaitasya nidaršanam ||108||

By having the darsan of Sri Rama in the forest, numerous Rshis were thus purified. By meditating on the (unique universal single) reality. This is the vindication of Advaita.

Matangavana ahûtâ<u>h</u> nadyas sapta ca sâgarâ<u>h</u> |
***cintite tapasâ*[11] ceti advaitasya nidaršanam ||109||**

The rivers and the seven seas were called to the Matanga forest just by remembering them by force of tapas. This is the vindication of Advaita.

Tapah prâdhâniko granthah samvâdo'yam tapasvinoh |
tapaso vighnakrd râjâ dukhabhâk putrakâranât ||110||

The whole Ramayana has its emphasis on tapas. It was itself a conversation between two tapasvis. By being the cause of stopping the tapas (of the Rshi couple and their beloved son) the King (Dasaratha) obtained total misery through his son's (separation).

Tapodrshtyâ srshtam idam šrîrâmâcca tapomayât |
utpattih šruta ity etat advaitasya nidaršanam ||111||

The entire Ramayana is a creation from the viewpoint of Tapas. By the fullness of the tapas of Sri Rama it is said to have had its origin. This is the vindication of Advaita.

Svânubhûtyaikamânam yat sushuptâvupalabhyate |
nânyat kimcillabhyate ca advaitasya nidaršanam ||112||

The experience of Self-hood that is available in deep sleep and (the fact) that nothing else is available then is the vindication of Advaita.

ArcitoVham tvayâ bhaktyâ[12] **samšitavratayâ hrdi |**
ityuktâ šabarî ceti advaitasya nidaršanam ||113||

I have been (properly) propitiated by you because of your having treasured me in your heart to the extent of freezing me there – thus was told Sabari. This is **the vindication of Advaita.**

Dehâtpravrajitair eva dehamityânubhûyate |
adrsye lînatâmetîty advaitasya nidaršanam ||114||

Only by (mentally) leaving the body one experiences the illusoriness of the body. (It is thus that) one merges in the Unseen Absolute. This is **the vindication of Advaita.**

Hitvâ dehâdi jîrnam yat avikârî ay at padam |
pašyanti sûraya iti advaitasya nidaršanam ||115||

Leaving the dead body and its associates, the great souls see the Immutable Absolute. This is **the vindication of Advaita.**

Jvalatpâvakasankâšam[13] **tâpasîrûpam âsritâ |**
svânanyam svargam eveti advaitasya nidaršanam ||116||

In the midst of the flames of fire did the ascetic woman bodily rise to the heavens. This is **the vindication of Advaita.**

Yatra te sukrtâtmânah viharanti maharshayah |
samâdhinâ labhyam[14] **iti advaitasya nidaršanam ||117||**

That one can achieve by Samâdhi what the great Rishis, souls of Merit, revel in, is **the vindication of Advaita.**

Deham evâdi sampâdya šokâvishto hy abhût kila |
pampâtîre râma iti advaitasya nidaršanam ||118||

Even Rama, by his association with the body was immersed in grief, on the shores of the river Pampa. This is **the vindication of Advaita.**

Svamâtmânam mahâtmânam[15] **vijâniyâd vicakshanah |**
mrtyuh sankucitam jnânam iti lakshmanabodhitah ||119||
Vijnâya svâtmano'dvaitam râmo dhairyam upâgamat |
âtmaikyajnânam advaitam balotsâhâdibhadradam ||120||

The wise man ought to wake up to his Inner Reality, the great Overself. Knowledge that is truncated (otherwise), is death. When Lakshmana recalled Him (to this realisation), Rama, coming back to the consciousness of the non-dual Self, regained his courage. Knowledge of non-duality of the

Self confers the best strength, the best enthusiasm, the best of everything.

> **Râmadagdha<u>h</u> kabandhašca šivam panthânam uktavân |**
> **sugrîvašca šubhâcara<u>h</u> <u>r</u>šyamûkena dhârita<u>h</u> ||121||**
> **Tena sakhyam ca kartavyam tadbhayasya nivâranât |**
> **tasya mâhâtmyam uktam ca bhâvikâryasya sûcanât ||122||**

Kabandha whose body was cremated by Rama, gave out the right path: 'Sugriva, who lives in Risyamuka, is good; you should make friendship with him, by removing his fears'. By indicating the future (potentialities) through him, his greatness was also told (by Kabandha).

> **<u>R</u>syamûkanivâsârha<u>h</u> sugrîva iti sevita<u>h</u> |**
> **pâpî vâlîti nišcitya na tatsevâm arocayat ||123||**

By the very fact that he deserved to stay in Risyamukha, Sugriva was sought by Rama. (By the same token), Vali was identified as a sinner and as such Rama did not want to seek his help.

> **Abhishicya ca sugrîvam râmah prašrava<u>n</u>e girau |**
> **giriš<u>r</u>ngam idam ramyam ramyajnânaikahetukam ||124||**
> **Iti šrimâtu<u>h</u> pûjâyâm šârade navarâtrake |**
> **udyukto munibhis sârdham parâšaktimayo'bhavat ||125||**

On the hills of Prasravana, Sugriva was coronated by Rama. This beautiful mountain peak is the best place for (seeking) spiritual illumination. So thinking, Rama, along with the Rishis, started the (Ritual) worship of Mother Godess in the autumnal navaratri and became One with Her Supreme Splendour.

ENDNOTES FOR PART 2

[1] V.R. 3 - 6 - 3

[2] V.R. 3 -9 - 30

[3] V.R. 3 - 9 - 33

[4] The Gita II -19

[5] V.R. 3 - 37- 13

[6] 3 - 39 -15

[7] The Gita 12 - 15

[8] V.R. 5 - 17 - 25

[9] Srimad Bhagavatam 10 - 2 - 24

[10] V.R. 3 - 74 - 22

[11] V.R. 3 - 74 - 25

[12] V.R. 3 - 74 - 31

[13] V.R. 3 - 74 - 33

[14] V.R. 3 - 74 - 35

[15] V.R. 4 - 1 - 125

PART – 3

Râmaikabhakto vîrašri hanûmân angul̤îyakam |
râmanâmânkitam gr̤hya vanditvâ prasthitah kapih ||126||

To Sri Hanuman the Great, Sri Rama was supreme. He received the ring with the imprint of Sri Rama's name, bowed and departed.

Kasthâmr̤tam yad advaitam pibed yo vîryavat tamah |
iti jnânaišvaryabalam adbhutam ca hanûmatah̤ ||127||

Hanuman has drunk the nectar of Non-duality rooted in the Supreme Brahman and this spiritual wealth makes his miraculous strength superlative.

Umâ haimavatî sthânam anvesht̤avyam mumukshubhih̤ |
advaitâ brahmašaktir yâ sakshâdrâmaprabheti ca |
ananyabhaktilabhyeti sundare ca pradaršyate ||128||

All seekers must look for the abode of Uma Haimavati, the Mother Goddess[1], the non-dual Cosmic energy personified as the brilliant lustre of Rama. That this will be achieved only by an unswerving devotion is being shown in Sundara-Kanda.

Sûryendrapavanâdinâm jyotiraikyam upeyushâ |
hanûmatâ svasârvâtmyam sphut̤am ca prakat̤îkr̤tam ||129||

It has been (already) shown by Hanuman, who sought (as a child) to reach the Oneness of the Power behind The Sun, Indra, Wind-God and others, thus demonstrating his own prowess.

**Mukteshuvat prasthito'yam lakshyam uddiśya dhîradhîh |
advaitaśaktipûrnatvât na glânim adhigaccati ||130||**

Like an arrow that has been discharged (from the bow) the brave Hanuman flew towards the goal. Being full of the energy of non-duality (of the Supreme) he never faltered.

**Giryâkârasya samkshobhât kapir dehavilakshanah |
darśanâdarśane hitvâ svayam kevalarûpatah ||131||
Advaitam brahma hanumân ajnânâm bhâti dehavat |
manasaiva krta lankâ nirmitâ viśvakarmanâ ||132||**

Giving a jolt to the gross form of the mountain, Hanuman, different and distinct from his body, threw off the seen and the unseen (matter-of-fact) universe and became his own Self. Hanuman shows the non-dual Brahman for the ignorant, just as the gross body (inferentially) points (the subtle body within), created by the Mind, the Visva-karma who created Lanka.

**Dîyamâneva câkâśam drśyate lingadehavat |
tatpraveśo yogaśaktyâ lankâkramanam ucyate ||133||**

It floats, as it were, in space, just as the subtle body (floats in space). By the powers of Yoga, if one enters it, that is said to be the jump to Lanka.

**Parâśaktiśca vividhâ hy asmâkam śrûyate kila |
upasamhrtya vividhâh manastattvâya kevalam ||134||**

The supreme Energy is said to have manifold manifestations. But they are only in the Mind-Principle.

**Dhîvrittîr yunjate viprâh pûrnâ ye deśakâlatah |
vastutas câpi pûrnatvam amrtattvam gatâ iti ||135||**

Viprâ ṛtajnâ amṛtâḥ bṛhataš câpi vipašcitaḥ |
nityam šuddham vastutattvam bhâvayantaḥ sadâ hṛdi ||136||

Those wise, who yoke (the totality of) the goings-on of their Intellect to the Fullness beyond Time, Space and Matter, are said to have reached Immortality. They are the Brahmins. They know the Cosmic Rhythm. They are immortal, great and learned. They always nurture in their hearts the truth of the Permanent and the Pure.

Sarvâdhishṭânam advandvarâmajyotis sanâtanam |
yat tadadrešyam agrâhyam tadevâmṛtam ucyate ||137||

By Immortality is meant that which is unindicatable and unamenable to the senses and which is the Eternal Light of the non-dual Rama which is the base of all there is.

Tad evâsritya hanumân sarvam karma karoti ca |
tadeva pašyan sarvatra râmânandânubhûš sada ||138||

Hanuman's refuge is That and That alone. All his actions are done that way. He sees That alone. He sees That everywhere. He experiences the Bliss of Rama all the time.

Dushkaram kṛtavân karma[2] **iti šlâghitavaibhavaḥ |**
sûkshmadehe praveše ca lankayâ dvâri vâritah ||139||

(Naturally) he is spoken of as having achieved the impossible. And when he enters the subtle body (Lanka) he is prevented at the gate by Rakshasi (Lanka).

Ahamkâras cakravartî tadbalair abhirakshitâ |
âjnânuvartinî lankâ tâm ca *nirjitavân*[3] hariḥ ||140||

Lanka is protected by the forces of Emperor Ego. (Rakshasi) Lanka is only his servant. Hanuman wins her over.

Lingadeham vikramitum râmašaktim samâšritah |
râvaṇasyâpi yâ šaktih svarâjyaparipâlane ||141||

To traverse the Lingadeha (subtle body) one has to fall back on the Sakti of Rama. The power of Ravana himself in governing his kingdom goes back to that source.

Sarvatrânusyûtatayâ ekaiveti ca gîyate |
ekâ satî dršyate ca nartakî dyoti tatprabhâ ||142||

Because of its universal immanence it is declared as One and One only. Its splendour shows up as the only Existence and shines as the Danceuse (Mâyâ)

Sraddhâbhaktidhyânayogât kaišcid evam hi budhyate |
nâsmâkam kart*r*tâ loke iti yo veda dhîradhî_h_ ||143||

Some realise it by the Yoga of Faith, some by the Yoga of Devotion, some by the Yoga of Meditation. Those who know that the Doership is not ours (but that of this Power) are the brave souls.

Sarvam apy avakâšam sa vicityâpi na d_r_sh_t_avân |
punastatpadaman vesh_t_um sîtârâmaprasâdata_h_ ||144||
tacchaktibhûtân devâmšca namask_r_tya svabhûtatah |
ekâm šaktim yad advaitam pradhy âtum upacakrame ||145||

Having searched every nook and corner, still he did not see the Mother. He again proceeded, by the Grace of Sita-Rama Himself, to look for Her. Bowing to the deities who derive their Powers from that Ultimate he sought to reach that One Non-dual Energy Source.

Šimšupâv_rksham âruhya sîtâvaibhavam âsthita_h |
svašaktisandhyâdhyânâya hy âgamishyati jânakî ||146||

Climbing the Simsupa tree, fixing his attention on the Glory of Mother sita, he knew she would come there to reflect upon Her own Sakti, that is, Sandhya.

Ityašokavanam prapya sîtâm d_rshtvâ mumoha ca |
svapaurushe_na d_rsh_tam yat sîtâsatyam tad adbhutam ||147||

Thus he reached the Asoka forest, saw Sita and was bewildered. This wonder that he saw as the Reality of the Mother has been the result of his own Inner Conviction (of non-duality).

Svapâtivratyamahimnâ svayam srîmâtr rûpata_h |
dašânanam ca dikk_rtya upadish_tavatî satî ||148||

By the power of Her own chastity, being Herself the Mother, she showed Her disgust of Ravana and gave him a piece of Her mind.

Ananyabhaktimatsîtâ vaidehi bhûmijâ parâ |
hanûmatâ samâšvastâ *aum ham hanûmate nama_h*[4] ||149||
Ham ity ekâkshare_naiva prak_rter jaya ishyate |
tîrtvâ mohâr_navam câpi dehabuddhyâtiga_h sadâ ||150||

The unswervingly devoted (to the Supreme) Sita, the princess of Videha, the daughter of the Earth, the Supreme (by Herself) was well-consoled by Hanuman. Well may we say Om Ham Hanumate namah, (to propitiate Hanuman). By the single syllable 'ham' one transcends the 'I-am-the-body' feeling and crossing the ocean of delusion achieves the victory over Prakriti, Cosmic Nature.

Hanûmân ṛkshasugrîvau gajo gṛdhro vaṇikpathaḥ |
svayambhûr nâradaḥ šambhuḥ kumâraḥ kapilo manuḥ ||151||
prahlâdo janako bhishmo balir vaivasvataḥ šukaḥ[5] |
ete samyakdṛshṭinishṭhaḥ svâtiriktâ'sahâ iti ||152||

Hanuman, the bear Jambavan, Sugriva, the elephant-king, the tradesman-traveller, Brahma, Narada, Siva, the boy Subrahmanya, Kapila, Manu, Prahlada, Janaka, Bhishma, Bali, Yama, and Suka – these are the Seers who see it right. They will not stand something other than the Self.

Sâkshyavasthâvyavahṛtau râmakṛshṇâdayo yathâ |
svasvarûpân na cyavante cidambarašarîriṇâḥ ||153||

(Recall that) Sri Rama and Sri Krishna dwelt only in the state of being a Witness, never slipped from Selfhood and had the entire space of Consciousness as their body.

Swâmimudrânkitakaraḥ sîtâšokavinâšanaḥ |
višvâsârtham ca sîtâyâḥ šrîrâghavaguṇâḥ šubhâḥ ||154||
uktâ šrîmaddhanumatâ dattam câpy anguḷîyakam |
na hi tvâm prâkṛtam manye[6] iti vîraḥ prašamsitaḥ ||155||

(Such) superlative qualities of Sri Rama were narrated by Hanuman to Sita, in order to generate the trust in him, who had with him the ring with the Lord's imprint on it and who had come to eradicate the misery of Sita. He gave Her the ring and was naturally praised by Her 'You are not an ordinary person'.

Avastu svamukham dṛshtvâ darpaṇe pratibimbitam |
tilakâdir dhâryate ca tathaiva vyavahâryate ||156||

The non-real body looks at its reflected image in the mirror and uses it to decorate the forehead. So also is worldly action.

**Yathâ sthite jagaty eva pûrnâtmânubhavo yatah |
vyavahâroVpi sulabhah acyutasya mahâtmanah ||157||**

For the great one, who never falters and for whom the experience of the fullness of the Atman is valid even while in this world, worldly action becomes easy.

**Jnâninašca na sîdanti kartavyeshu ca karmasu |
râmâdvišishtah ko'nyo'sti ity advaitam ca bhâvayan ||158||**

The enlightened ones, dwelling in the non-duality of there being nothing else other than Rama, do not fail in the actions obligatory on them.

**Maniratnam copagrhya hrdayenaiva tam gatah |
iti tâdâtmyabhâvena gamanâya matim dadhe ||159||**

Receiving the Chudamani from Her, he immediately merged in his mind with that Supreme; and in that mood, he decided to return (to Rama).

**Ahireva hy aheh pâdân âtmâ veda šubhâšubham |
iti sîtârâmagîte samyojyâdvaitabhâvanam ||160||**

Only the snake knows the snake's 'feet'. The Atma knows (what is) good and (what is) bad. This synthesis of the Sita Gita (spoken to the Rakshasis, in the Sundarakanda) and Rama Gita (spoken to Bharata in Ayodhyakanda) leads to the awareness of Non-duality.

**Eka eva par ohy âtmâ iti pârokshadaršanam |
âtmaikyajnânagîtena mahadyuddhe pravartitah ||161||**

Atman is one and one only. It is supreme. This is the mystic realisation. It is with this declaration and the wisdom of One-ness that Hanuman enters the Great War (with the

Rakshasas). (And we have to enter the world to wage the war with our senses and Ahamkara).

Nâtmanah kâmakâro[7]'stîty âtmavân šokatârakah |
Âšvâsya bharatam râmah šocyâšocyavivekatah ||162||

No individual is free to act on his own. Only the identity with the Self removes misery. This was the consolation given to Bharata by Rama by means of a discrimination between what to worry about and what not to worry about.

**Pratyagâtmam imam dharmyam satyam pašyanšca râghavah |
karmanâm karmabhûmau ca devâ hi phalabhâginah ||163||**

The truth of this Inner Reality was seen by Rama. On this action-centred Earth (even) the deities share the fruits of actions.

**Âtmâ nishkâma ity eva kâryam karma karoti yah |
pravartayan lokayâtrâm kâryâkâryavicakshanah ||164||**

The Atman is desireless. That is how one does actions in his pilgrimage through this world-life, discriminating between what ought to be done and what ought not to be done.

**Dharmam caranto dhîmantah ekabhâvam samâšritah |
vaideham sukham abhyasya jânanti sarvatah svayam ||165||**

The brave souls observe the (Laws of) Righteousness, having recourse to this attitude of One-ness. Practising the bodiless bliss they recognise the Self everywhere and by every means.

**Tasmât pâdân ahešcâpi ahir vettum tathârhati |
svaceshtitâni svasyaiva dhîvrittyâ viditâni hi ||166||**

Therefore it is that the feet of the snake are known only to the snake. Actions done by oneself are known only to the goings-on of one's own intellect.

Ko'nyo jnâtum prabhavati manasâ budhyate mana<u>h</u> |
dhiyaiva dhîvikârâšca grhyante ca yathârthata<u>h</u> ||167||

How can anyone else know it? Only mind understands (the same) mind. By intellect alone is seen the transformations of the intellect.

gaganam gaganâkâram[8] **ity advaitaviniščaya<u>h</u> |**
sankalpenaiva sankalpâ<u>h</u> unmûlyante yathâvidhi ||168||

Space is the only likeness of space. This is a confirmation of non-duality. Mental resolves and actions are properly rooted out only by mental resolves and actions.

Âtmaiva hy âtmano bandhu<u>h</u>[9] **ity advaitam parâm<u>r</u>tam |**
kimkarâšîti sâhasram jambumâlyâdi râkshasân ||169||
Hanûmân ekavîro'yam râmâdînâm anugrahât |
nig<u>r</u>hyâhamkârašatrum atyugrabalavân hari<u>h</u> ||170||
Sâkshâd ahamkârarâjna<u>h</u> sannidhâne ca nirbhaya<u>h</u> |
advitîyašca hanuman dharmam apy upadish<u>t</u>avân ||171||

The Atman is the only friend of the Atman. This is the supreme nectar of non-duality. All the enemies sent by the Emperor Ego – eighty thousand warriors, Rakshasas led by Jambumali, etc. – all were vanquished single-handed by the fierce Hanuman, by the Grace of Divinities Rama and Sita. Second-to-none, Hanuman arrived at the very presence of Emperor Ego face to face and without fear, he spoke words of wisdom.

Sarvalokešvaro râma<u>h</u> trilokî nâyakas tathâ |
ity ânjaneyavâkyam ca vibhîsha<u>n</u>oditam mahat ||172||

Rama is the Lord of the entire universe. He is the king of the three worlds (Bhuh, Bhuvah, Suvah; jagrat, svapna and sushupti; sattva, rajas, tamas; and the like). These words of Anjaneya were echoed by Vibhishana (also).

Sarvalokašaranyo'yam iti râma_h_ parâdvaya_h_ |
mahâtmeti ca pašyantau višvâmitravibhîsha_n_au ||173||

Rama is the only refuge for the whole universe. He is the non-dual supreme. He is the Mahatma. This was the insight of (both) Visvamitra and Vibhishana.

Sthiraprajno mahâtmeti nityasamšântarûpadh_rt_ |
iti vâlmîkivacanam advaitam sthâpayaty api ||174||

Valmiki's words: He is the man of firm wisdom; He is the Mahatma; He is the One who is ever at peace with Himself – also establish non-duality.

Dravîbhutaparâšaktipari_n_âmo hi râghava_h_ |
râmamâhâtmyavettâSyam hanumân šivavigraha_h_ ||175||

The supreme Cosmic Sakti Herself, in a melted form, is Rama. Hanuman who knows (this) greatness of Rama is Himself Siva in flesh and blood.

Srirâmâccapyananyo'yam tadajnâtvâ hi râva_n_a_h_ |
pucchasandîpanâkhyašca dan_d_o'yam kriyatâmiti ||176||
Sthûlasûkshmakâra_n_âkhyatraipureshvapi samsthitâ_h_ |
brahmâsvayambhûr[10]**ityâdi devâ yenâpi mohitâ_h_ ||177||**
Tam râmam evânubhûya harir dagdhvâ purîm api |
d_r_sht_â_ sîteti kishkindhâm âpa râmamana_h_ purîm ||178||

That this person is not any different from Sri Rama – was not realised by Ravana. Why, Even the Creator Brahma and other divines who are the deities stationed in the three bodies –

physical, subtle and causal – even they were confused by Him. Ravana ordered the burning of the tail, supposedly a punishment (to Hanuman). But the latter was steadfast in the experience of identity with Rama. He burnt up the whole city and reached Kishkinda with the cry: Seen is Sita.

Šrirâmasya parishvangah svatâdâtmyasya pûrnatâm |
advaitadyotako bhâvah vedya eva mahâtmabhi<u>h</u> ||179||

The embrace (that Hanuman had) with Rama indicates the fruition of the One-ness with the Inner Divinity. Only great souls experience this mood of Perfect Non-duality.

ENDNOTES FOR PART 3

52

[1] Kena Upanishad 3-12.

[2] V.R. 5 - 1 - 115

[3] Compare V.R. 5 - 4 - 1.The prefix 'ni' which is Valmiki's, indicates that not only there is victory but the vanquished comes to the victor's side.

[4] This is the mantra propitiating Hanuman.

[5] Srimad Bhagavatam 6 - 3 - 20

[6] V.R. 5 - 36 - 9

[7] V.R. 2- 105 - 15

[8] V.R. 6 - 110 - 24

[9] The Gita VI - 5

[10] cf. V.R. 5 - 51 - 44

PART – 4

Prârabdhakarmavegâcca na g̲r̲h̲n̲anti narâ hitam |
vibhîsha̲n̲asya yad vâkyam dhikk̲r̲tam râva̲n̲ena hi ||180||

Rarely does man listen to good advice. This is due to the force of Prarabdha (i.e. Karma that has begun to express itself through the *vasanas* created by it). How else did Ravana discard Vibhishana's words (of wisdom)?

Utpapâta gadâpâ̲n̲ih̲[1] **dharmâtmâ'yam vibhîsha̲n̲a̲h̲ |**
sarvâtmanâ s̲maran râmam vyuthânâvasare sthitam ||181||
Salakshmanam yadavastham šarîrârû̲d̲hatâ iti |
vettâ ya̲h̲ sarvabhâvânâm sârajnah purushasya hi ||182||

This righteous soul, Vibhishana, with mace in hand, (physically) rose in the skies, to the place where (the Lord) was with Lakshmana, remembering Rama from the innermost reaches of the heart. (This indicates esoterically that) Vibhishana was in the take-off position spiritually. Though embodied in a form, the Lord who knew all the minds, is actually the knower of the core of Purusha.

Vibhîsha̲n̲asya h̲r̲dvettâ antaryâmitayâ mahân |
sarvâbhayapradâteti tameva šara̲n̲am gata̲h̲ ||183||
Prapadye hyaksharam devam *ajarâmaram avyayam*[2] |
iti nairgu̲n̲yatejo yat šara̲n̲am na ja̲d̲asya hi ||184||

**Šrîmân gartasado râmah šanno astviti rakshitâ |
navo navo'yam madhura͟h _šrîrâma͟h_ _šara͟nam mama_[3] ||185||**

The great Lord knows the mind of Vibhishana. He gives Abhaya (Asylum through Fearlessness) to every one. Therefore it is that Vibhishana surrendered to Him. He is imperishable, He ages not. He is immortal. He is changeless. This is the splendour that is talked about as attributeless. To Him we should surrender, not to an inert physical form. The auspicious Lord, seated in His Chariot (of Perfection) (declares): Let there be only Bliss. And this protects you. Moment after moment He is sweeter. Let Sri Rama be my only refuge.

**_Angu͟lyagre͟na tân hanyâm_[4] iti lokottaram maha͟h |
sarvâbhibhâvî yat teja͟h ekameva yad advayam ||186||**

Just by lifting one little finger I'll kill them all. What an excellent prowess! This glory which overpowers everything and everybody is only the one without a second.

**Yâ yâ buddhir jâyate te dharmish͟tha bhavatu svayam |
iti tasya varo datta͟h amaratvam ca punyata͟h ||187||**

Whatever strikes the mind let it be, by itself, in concordance with Dharma. This had been the boon conferred on Vibhishana, along with a holy immortality.

**Iti tasya sahâyena samûlam rava͟no hata͟h |
jagatsarvam šarîram te sthairyam te vasudhâtalam ||188||**

Therefore it is that through his help Ravana was vanquished, along with all his roots. You, Rama, has the whole world as your body and your firmness is (like) the surface of the earth.

Tvam yajnastvam vashatkarah iti brahmagirâ harih |
ekameva yad advaitam sthâpitam vyavahâratah ||189||

You are the Yajna; You are (also) the deity of the Yajna – so sing the Vedas. The fact that there is One and only One without a second is thus an established maxim.

Vadhyo'yam manujeneti mânusham deham âšritah |
na tu tûshnîm avasthânam prabhuh kutrâpy arocayat ||190||

This demon had to be exterminated only by a human; thus it was that the Lord took to a human form. Never did the lord want to keep watching the situation silently.

Saputrâm tvâm tyajâmîti šâpas tâm na spršed iti |
ramena prârthito râjâ svapitâStra vimânagah ||191||

The father (Dasaratha) appeared in a vimana; he had earlier vowed to discard Kaikeyi along with her son and that the latter should not even touch (his body). Rama prayed to the father (to withdraw this curse).

Samutthâsyanti harayah nîrujo nirvrnâ api |
ityâdayo varâ bhadrâh prâptâ ramena šaktitah ||192||

All the monkeys would come back to life without pain, without wounds and without injury. Such were the pleasing boons obtained by Rama by his prowess.

Ahnâ tvâm prâpayishyâmi[5] ity evam prasthito harih |
navâyatanapûjârtham devâh sampâditâ iti ||193||

I will take you to Ayodhya in a single day – on this assurance of Vibhishana, the Lord left for Ayodhya where the divines who, having accomplished their objective, were now ready to offer the worship of the nine-seated Divinity[6].

Mânase *ratnapîthe*[7] **ca** *mânishâdapratishṭayâ*[8] |
vâlmîkiprârthito devaḥ navâyatanavaibhavât ||194||

In his mental frame Valmiki had already installed the almighty Narayana (Mâ-nishâda = Šrî-nivâsa) in the gem-studded seat of his mind and prayed to Him. This itself is due to the Glory of the Navâyatana (= the nine-seated Divinity).

Pûjyahšrîrâma eveti ahobhâgyamahodadhiḥ |
svarâjye vasa lankâyam iti rangavimânadaḥ ||195||

What an ocean of fortune (to Vibhishana)! Sri Rama is the only Ultimate to be worshipped. (With this goal of his), he was asked to stay in his own kingdom Lanka and was given the aereal seat (of the Lord Ranganatha)

Lankaišvaryam sukham bhunjan adhṛshyašca surair api |
adyâpy âste sukhî râjâ dharmâtmâyam vibhîshaṇaḥ ||196||
Aidam yugînair na dṛšyah iti câritram adbhutam |
yauvarâjye ca bharataḥ abhishikto mahân iti ||197||

Even today the good soul Vibhishana lives there as King, enjoying the bounties of Lanka and unassailable even by the divines. It is indeed mysterious that he cannot be seen by people of this Yuga. And, finally, Bharata was coronated as crown prince.

Shoḍašastambhasâhasramanṭape samavasthitaḥ |
advaitâmṛtavarshiṇyâ vâṇyâ sâkshâddhanûmate ||198||
Paramâdvaitatattvam yat bodhitam ṛshisanghake |
samam tattvam iti yat dvaitâdvaitavivarjitam ||199||

Seated in the majestic hall of sixteen thousand pillars, in the presence of the assemblage of rshis, he preached to none else than Hanuman, by words which spelt out a rain of nectar of the Oneness (of the Supreme), the central philsophy of

Absolute Advaita that is the equipoise, devoid of both duality and non-duality.

> **Râjnâm šatatrayam dṛshtvâ râmo madhuravâk svayam |**
> **yushmâkam cânubhâvena tejasâ ca mahâtmanâm ||200||**
> **Hato durâtmâ durbuddhî râvaṇo râkshasâdhamaḥ |**
> **hetumâtrama ham tatra bhavatâm tejasâ hataḥ ||201||**
> **Ity ahamkârariktena hṛdisthena mahâtmanâ |**
> **prajâmšca ranjayan vâkyam uktam šrotṛmanoharam ||202||**

Rama addressed the three hundred kings assembled before him and said: It is by your good wishes, your prowess, that the worst of the Rakshasas, the evil-minded sinner Ravana has been vanquished. I have been only the instrument. It is by your Glory that he has been killed. By such a self-effacing statement from the heart is Rama considered the greatest of men. And such words were not only pleasing to hear but also enthused the whole populace.

> **Advaitânubhavo loke sukhahetur mahâtmanâm |**
> **dvitîyavastubhânam yat putradârâdishu svayam ||203||**
> **Bhayašokâdihetušca advaitam tata âšrayet |**
> **gajânano nṛsimhašca somâskandâdivigrahâḥ ||204||**
> **Ardhanârîšvarâdîmšca samâšrity aikabhâvataḥ |**
> **bhindyâcca hṛdayagranthim bhedabuddhim tyajet sudhîḥ ||205||**

The becoming into a state of non-duality is the road to the happiness of great souls. When there is a perception of a second object, like son, spouse, etc., then it is that a cause for fear and grief arises. That is when one turns to Non-duality (as a cure). The multitudes of idols, Gajanana, Nrisimha, Somaskanda, Ardhanarisvara all have to be seen as One. The concept of difference has to be discarded by the wise. Thus let the knot of the mind be broken.

Advaite paramo dharmah pṛthivî ca pratishthita |
lokapîdâkaram karma râjasûyah šrutastviti ||206||
Svâtiriktâšvamedhena sarvahud yajna ishyate |
ity avyayo yad akshayyah dharmasetuh pratishthitah ||207||

The supreme dharma as well as the Earth itself stand on the foundation of Advaita. The Rajasuya yajna is heard of as a ritual which is exacting. In reality the yajna is a sacrifice of everything that is not the Self. This is the immutable, imperishable bridge of Dharma (leading to Enlightenment)

Brahmânumodito granthah râghaviyah parastviti |
gâyatryâšca svarupo yah satyajyotihpradah šubhah ||208||
Bharjakah svâtiriktasya gamakah svapadasya yah |
paramâdvaitasâmrâjyašriprado hy ayam eva tat ||209||

The supreme scripture is that pertaining to Rama, approved by Creator Brahma himself. It has the esoteric form of Gayatri built into it. It leads to the Light of Truth. The syllable Bha stands for the eradication of everything that is non-Self. The syllable ga takes you to your Real Nature. This is what gives the Bounty of the Kingdom of Supreme Non-duality.

Saccidghanâtmakajyotih râmachandra itîritah |
tatprabhâ prakṛtih sîtâ šrîmâtâ laliteti ca ||210||

The Light of the fullness of Existence, Knowledge, Bliss is Lord Ramachandra. The spark from that is the Prakriti, that is Sita also called Mother Goddess Lalita.

**Šaktišaktimator aikyam vedašâstreshu sammatam |
svâtantryenâVsatî sîtâ trikâlam râmam âšritâ ||211||**

The unity of Energy and the Source of Energy has been accepted by all scriptures. Sita therefore was not dependent. She always rests in Rama.

**Sakshâd râmamay*i* šakti_h_ advaiteva vij_r_mbhate |
ekaiva bhidyate bhrântyâ mâyayâ na svarûpata_h_ ||212||**

The power or energy which is nothing but the pervasion of Rama Himself is what exhibits itself as the non-dual One. The One, by a mysterious Mâyâ, looks varied, (which is) not so in reality.

**Sitâpratîtî râme_n_a tena bhâti carâcaram |
d_r_šyamâne jagaty asmin katham râmah pratîyate ||213||**

To Sri Rama all the movable and immovable universe shines as (Prakriti) the image of Sita. How can He believe in this visible universe ?

**Râmad_r_shtau jagannâsti jagadd_r_shtau na râghava_h_ |
rajjud_r_shtâvahir nâsti rajjur nâsty ahidaršane ||214||**

When Rama is seen, no universe is seen. When the universe is seen (as the universe) no Rama is seen. When the rope is seen there is no snake; when the snake is seen there is no rope.

***Râmabhûtam jagad abhût râme râjyam prašâsati*[9] *|
iti prâcetasî vâ_n_î advaitam ca pravarshati ||215||***

When Rama was ruling, the universe was full of (the fullness of) Rama -- wrote the ancient poet (Valmiki), thus proclaiming Advaita.

Râmamâtram jagad iti râma evâvašishyate |
tasminnâropitam višvam na tataḥ pṛthag eva hi ||216||

The universe is Rama alone. (After every non-real thing is discarded) Rama alone remains. It is on Rama that the 'universe' is superposed. It is not different from Rama.

Râmavṛksham raṇe hanmi ceti râvaṇajalpitam |
brahmavṛksham dyotayati advaitam yatparâmṛtam ||217||

Ravana blabbered: I will uproot the entire Rama-tree. The Brahman -tree is what is lighted by the Supreme nectar of Advaita.

Jyotirmayam yad advaitam *vâtam vanagatam yathâ*[10] |
***dadṛšuste na vai râmam*[11] *dahantam arivâhinîm*[12] ||218||**

What is non-dual and what is full of (the Supreme) effervescence is like the wind occupying the (whole) forest. (Recall how) the Rakshasa did not see Him spitting out fire (but they only saw the havoc caused by the fire).

Dṛshṭvâ râmasahasrâṇi gândharvâstreṇa mohitâḥ[13] |
***indriyârtheshu tishṭantam bhûtâtmânam iva prajâḥ*[14] ||219||**

The Core Force (Moola-bala) of Ravana, were stupefied by the Gandharva-astra of Rama and saw thousands of Rama's, (but not the source of them all) just as people (do not recognise the Jivatma which is the power-source for) all sense-experience of objects.

***Punaḥ pašyanti kâkutstham ekameva mahâhave*[15] |**
dadṛšû râmacakram tat kâlacakram iva prajâḥ ||220||

After the confusion, they again see the single Rama in that great war. This Rama syndrome was seen by them as people see the Time-syndrome.

Janamohanakaram rûpam sarvâkarshaṇašaktimat |
svîkṛtya bhagavân râmaḥ advaitam tattvam ûcivân ||221||

Lord Rama assumed the most attractive form which had the power of enticing all people. It was in this form that he spoke out the Advaita philosophy.

Satyam vastu sadopâsyam yadeva madhurâksharam |
râmeti madhurâ vâṇî sîtayâ ca šivena ca ||222||
Vâlmîkinâ vašishṭhena kapinâ cânubhûyate |
nânâ nishidhyate šâstre râma eko rasaḥ smṛtaḥ ||223||

The Reality which is the sweetest word (Rama) is to be meditated on always. The experience of this delicious name Rama has enchanted Sita, Siva, Valmiki, Vasishta and Hanumân. Rama is the only Essence – so say the Scriptures, denying all plurality.

JyotîrasoSmṛtam brahma[16] **râmanâmnâ virâjate |**
dehât parivṛjan neva râmam yâti ca nishkalam ||224||

By the name Rama what is declared is the Absolute Brahman which is the Light, the Essence, the Ultimate Nectar of Spirituality. Only by abandoning the I-am-thebody attitude, one reaches Rama, the faultless.

Ramâjjyotirmayâd anyat vastu nâstîti šastrataḥ |
asantam pratyupasthâpya janâḥ pašyanty avastukam ||225||

The scriptures proclaim that there is nothing real beyond the Glorious Light of Rama. Men on the other hand, place their faith in the non-real and see only the ephemeral things.

Dravasya pâyasasyeha râmâdy âkâratâ katham |
tatve vicâryama<u>n</u>e ca vispash<u>t</u>am na nirûpyate ||226||

Just from the pâyasa drink it is said that Rama and his brothers were born. If this is investigated to its logical conclusion truth will not show it right.

Indrajâlâdi d<u>r</u>sht<u>â</u>ntai<u>h</u> mâyaisheti nigadyate |
râmâdînâm janiścoktâ jâtâ iva bhavanty aho ||227||

Instances of shows of magic are known to be only appearances. By the same analogy the birth of Rama and others has to be analysed. It is as if they were born!

Avatâra rahasyam ca pancaślokaiśca[17] gîyate |
d<u>r</u>śyam nâstîti śrutyâ ca advaitam bodhyate khalu ||228||

The secret of the Lord's Avatara is sung in the Gita in five verses. Even the vedic statement that what is visible does not exist, teaches only non-duality.

Etad rûpam bhagavato hy arûpasya cidâtmana<u>h</u> |
mâyâgu<u>n</u>airviracitam tasya kriyâs tatheti ca ||229 |

The form of the Lord which is visible is only that of the formless Absolute Consciousness. It is the making of Maya and its gunas.

Anayâ śukavâ<u>n</u>yâ ca advaitatvasya jnaptaye |
lokarîtyâ dvaitakathâh tattvanirdhâra<u>n</u>âya hi ||230||

By these words the sage Suka reminds us of non-duality. Indeed all talk of duality in the ordinary world is to establish the ultimate principle.

Bhâvanâmâtram advaitam sanâtanasukhâtmakam |
svakarmasûtragrathite[18] **dvaitaloke ca mâyike ||231||**

The principle of non-duality is to be only in terms of attitude; that will be the essence of an eternal happiness in this non-real world of plurality where every life is strung in the string of one's own karma.

Yathânušishṭam kartavyam phaloddešam vinâ sadâ |
karmaṇyevâdhikâraste[19] **šastrîye vihitepi ca ||232||**

What has been prescribed has to be done (and that too) without any concern or expectation of the fruit of the action. Your right is only to do the work, (work which is) prescribed by the scriptures.

Dṛšyam na višvasanîyam iti mâyâmṛgâdayaḥ |
vidyujjihvendrajinmâyâḥ mâyâyuddhoSpi sarvataḥ ||233||

What is seen is not to be trusted ever; like the magical (golden) deer, like the mâyâs of Vidyujjihva or Indrajit and like the magic wars they fought.

Râmâdînâm mohakaryaḥ tathaivedam carâcaram |
tasmâcchrutyâ tathâ yuktyâ dṛshṭam sarvam parîkshayet ||234||

Even people like Rama were confounded; in the same way the whole mobile and immobile world (may be confounded). Therefore one should examine everything that is seen, with the help of scriptures and one's own logic.

Šântidântyâdikṛtayâ gurvanugrahato dhiyâ |
adṛšyam nirguṇam sûkshmam satyasatyam ca sarvataḥ ||235||

By actions (monitored by) patience and self-control and by intelligence (sanctioned by) the Grace of Guru (one should arrive) at the Unseen, the attributeless and the subtle which is the truth of truths.

Drshtvetarân upeksheta vidvân yaśca vicakshanah |
mâyâmrgam satyam iti grhîtva vanchitah prabhuh ||236||

The wise man ignores the inconsequential by scrutinising everything; the Lord (however) took the magic deer to be real and was deceived.

Mahâpatsu ca dhîrena kartavyam karma yacchubham |
sandhyopastyâ ca kâleshu svatattvam avadhâryatâm ||237||

Even in times of great danger, the wise have to do what is to be done; during the times of sandhya-upasana (at sunrise and sunset) one should reflect upon the Self embedded in oneself.

Nârînâm patireveha śaranam mukhyadharmatah |
pâtivratyamahâtejah rakshitavyam ca garbhavat ||238||

The most important Dharma for women is that their refuge is the husband. This principle of pâti-vratya should be treasured like a pregnancy that is treasured.

Pathyante râmavishayâh yatra yatreti mârutih |
pûrnânandanimagnaśca grantheshu śatakotishu ||239||

Wherever the subject of recitation is Rama, Hanuman is already there listening to it. He is immersed in the Bliss of that Eternally Perfect One and in the 100 crores of verses (about Him).

Ekam ca bhagavattattvam sarvatra pratipâdyate |
ity advaitaparâ vedâh smrtiśâstrapurânakâh ||240||

The One divine principle is what is reflected everywhere. This non-duality is the undercurrent of all vedas, smritis and puranas.

Râma eva sadâdvaita<u>h</u> gaganâkâra îšvara<u>h</u> |
bhûtâkâsâccidâkâša<u>h</u> yah sûkshmatama îrita<u>h</u> ||241 |

The Divinity Rama is pervading (the whole universe) like space; the space of consciousness is subtler than the world of the elements, so also is the subtlest concept (of the Ultimate One).

Sadârâmamayo bhûtvâ šivašaktyâtmakah pumân |
ramârpa<u>n</u>am idam šastram ramaparyâvasânata<u>h</u> ||242||

One should be full of Rama always. It is the fullness of Siva and Sakti. This work is (therefore) dedicated to Rama. All this merges in Rama.

Râmaya<u>n</u>âdvayam iti šrîrâmagurusevayâ |
râmoham aum tatsaditi *râm râmâya nama<u>h</u> svâhâ*[20] ||243||

Thus ends Ramayana-advayam, by the Grace of the Lord and the Guru, (with the incantations:) Rama am I, Om Tat Sat; Râm Râmâya namah svâhâ.

ENDNOTES FOR PART 4

[1] V.R. 6 - 16 -17

[2] Brihad-aranyaka-upanishad

[3] This is the famous eight-lettered (*Ashtâkšharî*) mantra of Rama.

[4] V.R. 6 - 18 - 23

[5] V.R. 6 - 124 - 8

[6] The *'Navayatana'* constituents are: Sita, Lakshmana, Bharata, Satrughna, Hanuman, Sugriva, Vibhishana, Angada and Jambavan.

[7] V.R. 6 - 131 - 60

[8] V.R. 1 - 2 - 15

[9] V.R. 6 - 131 -101

[10] V.R. 6 -94 -21

[11] V.R. 6 - 94 - 21

[12] V.R. 6 - 94 - 26

[13] Compare V.R. 6 - 94 - 26,27

[14] V.R. 6 - 94 - 23

[15] V.R. 6 - 94 - 27

[16] Veda mantra incorporated in the Pranayama ritual.

[17] The Gita IV -5 to 9

[18] Yogavasishtam: cf. *Sukhasya dukhasya na ko V pi dâtâ paro dadâtîti kubuddhir eshâ |*

aham karotîti vrithâbhimânah svakarmasûtragrathito hi lokah ||

[19] The Gita II - 46

[20] This is one of the sacred mantras for Rama.

****